A WORLD BEYOND MYSELF

Rutger Kopland
A WORLD BEYOND MYSELF

Selected poems translated from
the Dutch by
James Brockway

with a foreword by
Jeremy Hooker
and an introduction by the translator

London
ENITHARMON PRESS
1991

First published in 1991
by the Enitharmon Press
BCM Enitharmon
London WC1N 3XX

Distributed in the USA
by Dufour Editions Inc.
PO Box 449, Chester Springs
Pennsylvania 19425

Poems © Rutger Kopland, 1966, 1968, 1969, 1972, 1975
1978, 1982, 1985, 1989
Translations and Introduction © James Brockway 1991
Foreword © Jeremy Hooker 1991

ISBN 1 870612 81 7

ACKNOWLEDGEMENTS

The translator expresses his thanks to the editors of the following magazines for the support they gave in printing most of the poems included in this selection: *Stand Magazine, London Magazine, Encounter, The Spectator, Poetry Durham, Outposts Poetry Quarterly, Acumen, Foolscap, The Rialto, Iron, Envoi, Prospice, Poetry Wales, Sunk Island Review, PEN International* and to Jackson's Arm Press, which published the pamphlet *The Prospect and the River* in 1987.

Assistance from the Netherlands Fund for Translation is gratefully acknowledged.

Set in Bembo by Bryan Williamson, Darwen
and printed by
Billing and Sons Ltd, Worcester

Contents

Foreword 9
Introduction 13

From *Among Cattle* (1966)
A Psalm 17
Under the Apple Tree 18
Rowans 19
Walk with my Daughter 20
The Mare 21
The Turkeys 22
Hampstead Heath 23

From *Yesterday's Barrel-Organ* (1968)
Lost in the House 24
His Mac 25
A Long Walk 25
Miss A 27
Mr K 28

From *Everything by Bike* (1969)
Johnson Brothers Ltd 29
Our Gasworks 30
Still-Life 31
Young Lettuce 32
Ulumbo, a Cat 33

From *The Finder Hasn't Looked Properly* (1972)
The Man in the Garden 34
When, Where? 35
Against the Creaking Gate 36
For Bukovsky 37

From *An Empty Spot to Stay* (1975)
No Reply 38
No More Suffering 39
An Empty Spot to Stay 40
Crow 41
She Waits 42
Slowly, in Drops 43

From *All those Fine Promises* (1978)
    Father, I See your Face 44
    Who Are You? 45
    He Knows Why 46
    Painting 47
    Breughel's Winter 49

From *This View of Things* (1982)
    All Those Fine Promises 50
    The Surveyor 51
    Conversation 52
    Onwards 54
    Suppose 55
    Further 56
    In the Mountains 58
    A River 60

From *Before It Disappears and After* (1985)
    Bay 62
    What I Said 63
    The Valley 64
    Natzweiler 65
    Conversation with the Wanderer 67
    I Cavalli di Leonardo 68
    Ghiberti's La Porta del Paradiso 69
    Michelangelo's David 70
    Michelangelo's Cristo Deposto di Croce 71
    Rain and Wind 72

From *Thanks to the Things* (1989)
    Afternoon in the Country 73
    Portrait 74
    Portrait with Bride and Bridegroom 75
    Portrait with Dog 76
    Self-Portrait 77
    Horses 78
    Thanks to the Things 79

Foreword

When I read Rutger Kopland's poems certain places that I know and love come back into my mind, especially the woods and rivers and pastures of Drenthe, the province in the north of the Netherlands where the poet lives. Not only the places but also the seasons, effects of mist and light, and creatures, especially the horses: a whole living world that exists outside the poems but which the poems help me to savour and to see. But this is not to say that Kopland is a local poet in any narrow sense, although locality has entered deeply into his poetry. A reader may or may not know the places outside the poems – it doesn't matter; what the poems prove upon our senses is how real the world is, yet how little we know it.

The settings of Kopland's poems are not confined to Drenthe or even to the Netherlands. He is, however, distinctively a Dutch poet, and therefore a European poet; by which I mean that he, in common with other European poets and artists, conveys a strong sense of the special material and spiritual qualities that make his country unique. Rutger Kopland's poetic world, like Tomas Tranströmer's, expresses the reality of a particular place and time; but Kopland is not, any more than Tranströmer, a poet with a naive sense of what is real. There are marked differences between the Swedish poet and the Dutch poet, but they share an awareness of the depths of human subjectivity together with the conviction that the world is not primarily a psychological phenomenon, but radically *other*.

The certainty that the world really exists, and is prior to the artist's shaping mind, is one that Kopland shares with Vermeer and other Dutch masters. It is inevitable that in writing about Kopland's poetry, which often refers to paintings and photographs, I should note its visual qualities, and relate it to the great artistic tradition of his nation. This emphasis, however, would be wholly misleading if it were to suggest that Kopland is a painter in words, instead of what he really is, a fine lyrical poet with a gift for rhythm and poetic structure as well as imagery. Moreover, if the world in Kopland's vision is as substantial, as present, as it is in Vermeer's paintings, it is also as elusive, as profoundly enigmatic. Kopland shares with other artists, too, a sense of what art can and cannot show. He observes in one poem that the more Leonardo tried to depict how the horse is made, the more he realized that its living reality, its 'secret', was beyond him, and in another, that Michelangelo, at the end of his life, smashed his *Cristo Deposto di Croce* and left it incomplete. That incompleteness testifies to the great sculptor's humility in face of ultimate reality. Kopland, also, knows that the world is beyond him, and the reality of life eludes his words. One effect of his knowledge is that he has a heightened sense of human vulnerability and of the care we owe one another. Another effect is that he is able to intimate what he sees as the essentially elusive quality of the real.

Kopland is a metaphysical and might also be described as a religious poet, provided the word is not confounded with any orthodoxy. He is haunted by time and teased out of mind by eternity. He has intimations of a humanly impossible peace, and of the determined being possibly indetermined. The landscape of the twenty-third Psalm is one of his recurring motifs. Indeed, the green pastures and still waters, which were inextricably part of his childhood, merge with the Dutch landscapes of his poetry. But whether seen outside the barbed wire of the concentration camp in 'Natzweiler', or in 'this endearing landscape' in 'All Those Fine Promises', the image of the world restored in perfect peace and happiness does not provide the poet with answers. He sees 'eternal questions' playing around Christ's mouth. It is, perhaps, partly Kopland's knowledge as a psychiatrist – his knowledge of the irreducible in human suffering – that saves him from the temptation that besets many poets to project merely verbal resolutions. In any case, he questions sanely and humanely; he has no answers.

There is a strong celebratory impulse in Kopland's poetry, and he is capable of expressing happiness as well as melancholy. His poems about human relationships, between parents and children and between man and woman, are especially moving. Tenderness characterises his way of seeing and feeling generally, and he is also a love poet of sexual passion. As with other metaphysical poets, as different from him and from each other as John Donne and George Oppen, the domestic and familial world, in which his feelings are strongly involved, is also a focus of his questioning. Kopland is a subtle poet, a poet of intimations and implications, who is centrally concerned with the primary human and poetic theme of love and death. As he seems to say in 'Painting', there are, as it were, only two moments in the life of a human being: the departure of love that leaves only death, and the presence of love that is accompanied by death. As well as being a theme, Kopland's sense of the inseparability of love and death pervades all his seeing and feeling, and touches his tenderness with a life-enhancing chill and wonder.

There is, often, a stillness about Kopland's landscapes. But if his poems are still-life pieces, the stillness is deceptive, and is life-like by being quick with vital impulses that we may sense but cannot see. Denis Diderot, after his trip to Holland in 1772, wrote admiringly of Dutch industry and ingenuity. 'Wherever one goes in that country,' he said, 'one sees art grappling with nature, and always winning.' Even today, long after the lapse of Dutch trading supremacy, it is still tempting to see the Netherlands, manmade as it largely is, as a country in which art – in the widest sense of the word – triumphs over nature. The still-life paintings of the seventeenth century might provide an emblem of this condition: the products of nature brought to the table, arranged by human beings for human consumption. Of course, the best pieces have a wonderful freshness, and are cornucopias of the good life – even when they symbolise mortality. But the many lesser examples of the genre are suffocating and nauseating, offering a soulless, dead nature, with the touch of man's busy and acquisitive hands all over it. It is that sense of everything being known and handled by man that produces a depressing stereotype of the Netherlands.

The surveyor, in Rutger Kopland's poem of that title, is surrounded by a world that is 'perfectly clear' because 'everything has been observed'. On the face of it, it would seem that Dutch landscape would represent the experience of the surveyor, and stand for the comprehensively known and determined. But that is not the world of Rutger Kopland's poems, in which, in the words of 'Further', the maps have been left behind, because 'they told us what we already knew, / where we came from. / Not where we were'. His is a world in which the poet is 'on the point of going further / and not knowing how', indeed, 'not knowing what / anything means'.

For me, with little knowledge of Dutch, the poems are identified with the sensitive, faithful translations of James Brockway, who, with the publication of this selection, greatly enhances his already significant contribution to promoting knowledge of Rutger Kopland's poetry among English readers. One of the most memorable and attractive features of the poems is their depiction of a landscape at once fluid and open, with far prospects, which corresponds to the poet's sense of life's duality, and is also recognisably a Dutch landscape. When I read Rutger Kopland's poems certain places that I love come back into my mind, but imbued with a strangeness in the light of which the places are curiously more real. His is a poetry of things – occasionally, in a phrase or a perception, it is reminscent of William Carlos Williams. But the things and the world they belong to are essentially *other*, with a freshness and an elusive, enigmatic quality that feel more like life than products of art.

Jeremy Hooker

Introduction

The Dutch poet Rutger Kopland was born in 1934 and published his first volume of poems in 1966. In 1989 his ninth collection appeared, by which time he had become one of Holland's leading poets and one of the most widely read, his volumes going into several impressions. He had also become the recipient of three literary awards of distinction, including the P.C. Hooft Prize for 1988, his country's highest award for literary achievement.

During this period, his parlando voice, speaking to the reader in poem after poem, usually brief, has become instantly recognisable as his. At the same time, his poetry has undergone a considerable and significant development, moving from personal and sensitive reactions to life in a predominantly rural environment, impressions often anecdotal and ironical in tone, towards a more esoteric poetry of metaphysical and philsophical content, all couched in the simplest of pared down language.

In his later work, the poet has left behind him the past and the mental and spiritual security of an upbringing 'with the bible' in a relatively simple world and is often out, alone and without maps, on journeys of exploration in strange territory, in a spare landscape of the mind. Of poetry in general he has himself said that 'it is exploratory...it throws up questions...questions without answers.'

The translations in this selection from his work to date have been taken from all nine of his volumes so far, so that his progress can, to an extent at least, be followed here. Rather more emphasis has, however, been laid on the later poetry.

I took up the English translation of Kopland's poetry in 1983, five years before the award of the P.C. Hooft Prize was announced. By then Kopland already enjoyed a considerable reputation and popularity as a poet and had been much written about and interviewed. But it was not this that had attracted me to his work. Twenty years had passed since I had been closely concerned with Dutch writing and actively engaged in its translation, and in 1983 it was to Kopland's early work that I had been attracted – by reading articles about him which contained examples from his first collections.

These were the first poem in his first volume, the highly seminal 'A Psalm', in which the father of a young child looks back to his early childhood, 'Under the Apple Tree', likewise from his first collection, and 'A Long Walk' from his second. The strong appeal came from the voice I heard talking to me in these poems in a quiet parlando manner and from the fascination exercised by a relaxed style which might also be taken for prose but was, by virtue of the distinctive tone of voice and the mind behind that voice, indubitably poetry. It was free verse, unrhymed but with tonal echoes, from which the reader receives his sense of an individual form that Kopland has made his own. It was also a poetry of intimate human experience expressed in a language at the same time simple and subtle, devoid of all the usual devices of poetic rhetoric, and infused with a quiet, gentle irony, humour and melancholy.

The poem 'Under the Apple Tree' is as appropriate an example as any of the early work. It describes a man's coming home in the evening and sitting in his garden as the night falls around him. Besides creating, seemingly effortlessly, a remarkable sense of quiet, this poem also embodies, equally effortlessly, a philosophy of life.

From such beginnings, via periods when it has been erotic, even political, and at times charged with nostalgia for the past, Kopland's work has developed to become a spare poetry of metaphysical questioning. A questioning of received beliefs and concepts and even of our human perception of things.

Gradually everything seems called into question and especially the authenticity of what we think and see and feel – what we think we see and feel. This in turn develops into the wish to see the world and things as they really are in their independent existence and not as man sees them – a wish to disappear from the scene oneself, expressed explicitly in 'Conversation with the Wanderer'.

Here, I feel, we draw near to the poetry of Fernando Pessoa, especially in his persona as Alberto Caeiro. More than once when reading many of the later poems I have been reminded too of the world that confronts us in the paintings of the Belgian surrealist, René Magritte – a world in which things, still recognisable, have been re-arranged and juxtaposed by the imagination. In this world we are 'going forward without knowing how... without knowing what anything means', as Kopland himself puts it in his poem 'Further'. It is a poetry inspired by what Octavio Paz, writing of Fernando Pessoa's poetry, has termed 'the immanence of the unknown'. But Kopland's later poetry contains poems of a different nature too, as is witnessed by the four Florence poems, in which the poet reacts to the work of the great artists of the Italian Renaissance.

When translating Kopland's poems, it has always been my

endeavour to keep as close as the English language will allow to the original Dutch versions, while also reproducing as far as possible Kopland's mood, rhythms and tone. Time after time phrases which have strayed away from these have been restrained and brought back into line. Essentially, these are my translations but Kopland's poems.

Most of the translations collected here have appeared in English literary and poetry magazines since 1983 and all have been made in consultation with the poet himself. I dedicate them to the memory of Bram de Rouville de Meux, on whose invitation it was that I came to Holland many years ago.

James Brockway

A Psalm

The green pastures the still waters
on the wallpaper in my room –
as a frightened child I believed
in wallpaper

when my mother had said prayers for me
and I had been forgiven for one day more
I was left behind among
motionless horses and cattle,
a foundling laid in a world
of grass

now that once again I have to go
through god's pastures I find no path
to take me back, only a small hand
clasped in mine that tightens
when the enormous bodies
of the cattle grunt and snuffle
with peace.

Under the Apple Tree

I came home, it was about
eight and remarkably
close for the time of the year,
the garden seat stood waiting
under the apple tree

I took my place and sat
watching how my neighbour
was still digging in his garden,
the night came out of the soil
a light growing bluer hung
in the apple tree

then slowly it once again became
too beautiful to be true, the day's
alarms disappeared in the scent
of hay, toys again lay
in the grass and from far away in the house
came the laughter of children in the bath
to where I sat, to
under the apple tree

and later I heard the wings
of wild geese in the sky
heard how still and empty
it was becoming

luckily someone came and sat
beside me, to be precise it was
you who came to my side
under the apple tree,
remarkably close
for our time of life.

Rowans

To practise the art of poetry is
to state with the greatest possible care
that, for instance,
in the early morning
the rowan trees bear thousands of tears
like a drawing from childhood,
so red and so many.

Walk with my Daughter

She says, that is the wind
and points to the waving grass,
of a patch of light on the path
she says, this is the sun,

as though, through her, Creation has begun.

But if with my own two eyes I look
to where the sun and wind have been,
I see she comes up only
to my knees.

Daily out of my feet, exhaustlessly,
grows the giant in my own fairytale,
which is slowly becoming transparent
like a morning in the mist.

Step by step my seven league boots
are sending me down trails
I thought were lost to me,
the hard and tiny pebblestones
of young Tom Thumb.

The Mare

She bears the heavy equine flesh
wearily through the twilit fields
until, grey into grey, she disappears
between heaven and earth –
had her day   amen

but of a night I witnessed how
she rolled herself snorting through the grass
as though, mounted by the devil, she would
thrash the air to throw him off

and the morning after a poor night's sleep:
her head at the gate above the trough
oats on her chops
her mane awry
her eyelids halfway drawn
down rounded misty panes.

The Turkeys

They lend our neighbour's garden
where they come to spend
the Christmas holidays the allure
of an old English engraving.
Although grey ladies with on their heads
the congealed red tears
of a most distinguished grief,
they are even more inquisitive
than the chicken, of whom as they step,
all circumspection, along the paths,
they seem to be forever warning one another:
Remember – you're a turkey, dear.

Hampstead Heath

You were walking so stiff and pale
that I thought how tired you are
and lovable and you said how
fine a wood of birch trees only is
don't you agree

On Hampstead Heath it was still
that sort of winter that co-operates
gladly with any grief we have –
wind-still, misty, horizonless

I felt how the hair in your neck
and the fur on your overcoat
were moist and over your shoulder
I saw a woman out walking
her dogs alone.

On the death of my father

1. *Lost in the House*

Our begetter has left his descendants
for ever. My brothers and I
shorten the night in the heavy armchairs
he reserved for his guests, in the dark
suite of his memory.

But thank god he left a box
of cigars in his house,
the cellar's full of drink,
we're granted strength to bear our cross.

I bumped into him this evening, I say,
not the real him – more vigorous
and friendlier than before.
He greeted me hastily and went on his way,
in and out of rooms, as though he wanted
to go the rounds of his house
once more, before bolting it off
from the advancing night.

So lives and dissolves in words, smoke
and glass, a father, tangible as the ash
on our Sunday suits, but as lost,
as irrecoverable,
is our childhood, Lord bless
our forgetting.

2. *His Mac*

My father had only just died
when my mother carefully
took down his new macintosh
from the hat-stand. Try it on,
she said. He was so proud of it.

So there I stood and from
the sleeves and as I fastened
the buttons, I felt how dead he was,
and how far away my childhood. I should
grow weak and old and in these folds
my skin would start to sag
about my bones.

3. *A Long Walk*

Walking with my children B and R –
winter returns and slowly I'm wound
once more into the never-changing web
of misty woodlands, muddy tracks,
the chill shriek of pheasants,
the earth rumbles with a trio
of fjord horses, melancholy of
cabbage fields tinged with frost.

Everything changes yet comes back
unchanged. Take the saints of these months.
A child knows that St Martin leaves
with half a cloak and comes back with
a new one. St Nicholas is always
with us, though that we do not always see.
Mary walks with a new Jesus and again
she's nearing her time. Our world
turns out to be circular.

That's why we always arrive back at the same
trees, in which my daughters always climb the same
branches and waving from their crowns sing
the St Nicholas song, and look! how high we are!
And it's true they are beyond my reach,
should they fall I'd have to let them fall.

Walking towards home through the failing light,
we discuss the moon and grandpa's death.
They've just a morsel of sympathy
for me, for grandpa was my father. (He
it was who in those days, swathed in curtains,
with a beard of teased-out string down
to his knees, a wobbly mitre on his head,
crept through the moonlight for me.)

Walking in the dark, I feel
the cold of their hands, have to
carry their withered flowers,
blow their noses,
fasten their buttons,
be their father.

Miss A

On September 19, a misty
nineteenth, Miss A stepped off
from the wrong side of her house-boat
Sweet Content
into the waters of 'The Deep'.

The cold had come, she had been unable
to get the stove to light,
her old mother had died,
everything was creaking, going to rust,
from her galley God and the
DHSS seemed out of reach.

She disembarked.

Mr K

Mr K has now been removed to the asylum
for good, because every night he wanted
to go to mother. It no longer helped to say
that mother had died twenty years ago.
Five minutes later he climbed on the moped anyway
and vanished into the dark, full-throttle.

Mr K (51), his face stilled by sclerosis,
knows nothing now, he merely smiles towards the end
of the day as he looks outside and sees
it already becoming dark. Ah well, he says,
then I'll be getting on again.

Johnson Brothers Ltd

In those days when my father was still big,
dangerous tools in the bulging pockets
of his jacket, in his suits the odours
of teased out twine and lead,
behind his eyes the incomprehensible world
of a man, gas-fitter, first-class,
said mother, in those days how different
my feelings were, when he would shut the doors
on her and me.

Now he is dead and I am suddenly as old as he,
it turns out to my surprise that he too had
decay built into him. In his diary I see
appointments with persons unknown, on his wall
calendars with gas-pipe labyrinths,
on the mantelpiece the portrait of a woman
in Paris, his woman, the incomprehensible
world of a man.

Looking into the little hand-basin of porcelain
dating from the 'thirties, with its silly pair of lions,
Johnson Brothers Ltd., high up in the dead-still
house the sad shuffle of mother's slippers,
Jesus Christ, father, here come the tears
for now and for then – they flow together
into the lead of the swan-neck pipe,
no longer separable from the drops that come
from the little copper tap marked 'cold'.

Our Gasworks

Father, you left behind you
the most beautiful gasworks
on earth,

sheds with little rails
running under the doors, chimneys,
the house

we lived in. Colours of
coal and of coal-
ash,

silent and summery with grass
that blossoms and covers
everything over.

Still-Life

They can't be separated from
each other. Secrets are incurable:
the darkness under her skirts,
the shabby knickers when she died,
the knot found in his handkerchief,
the impotent member on his corpse.

Old man living with the portrait
of a woman, old woman living
with the portrait of a man:
the way they stared into a lens.

Young Lettuce

I can stand anything,
the shrivelling of beans,
flowers dying, I can watch
the potato patch being dug up
and not shed a tear – I'm
real hard in such things.

But young lettuce in September,
just planted, still tender,
in moist little beds, no.

Ulumbo, a Cat

Like us he had his
quirks, but more
indifference.

In the winter he loved
stoves, in summer
little birds.

Sick and as indifferent
to death as to us.
Dying he did himself.

The Man in the Garden

We think the animals have begun to speak again:
things had gone wrong with him once more.

He would sit in his chair in the garden and we
had to feed him. Peanuts and Pilsner. We loved him,

but our life together had been wrecked:
as long as we had known each other he'd been

at work digging up the dead. How good and kind
they were! We had to hear that more and more.

Now in his memories it was all success, everything
after all had gone well, he laughed as happy

as a sandboy. We couldn't bear to see it:
so young still and yet so old.

And just as dogs will whine when their boss
leaves home, so we whined when he left us,

en route to new adventures.

When, Where?

It's autumn and the dogs are at it again.
There's no tenderness among dogs.

Say something, she says. Only a child can know
what I feel. I'm a child no more.

Tenderness, that's, I say, as I take
her breasts firmly in my hands,

that's the answer to a question that's
not been asked. The odour of every autumn,

I mean, the question when, where
was it and the answer to that.

I can smell your hair again, we're sitting
against each other on a bench in the gardens.

I feel what a child feels when it sees
what we are doing. What we are saying is nonsense.

Against the Creaking Gate

And so we stood against the creaking gate,
as out of this world as horses are.

Again it was earth, muck, soir de paris,
an evening of where and when.

Forgotten verses surfaced inside me,
faint pastures, gentle, rhyming with night,

but you whispered: here, here it is
best, where you are now, where you are

with your hands. And so we lay pressed
to the earth and to each other, while the gate

creaked with importunate horses.

For Bukovsky

Hatred goes garbed like peaceful folk
in togas, tailored suits and corduroy.
Hatred looks very ordinary indeed.

Among your judges are world reformers,
the working class isn't waiting for you, but
for them. Like they're waiting, oh yes, for god.

Among your admirers are the respectable
salaried sleepers, who think it perfectly okay
to murder – not a fly but a people.

Hatred of people goes mostly garbed
in words of love for one's fellow men.

No Reply

Give me the broad, the languid rivers,
the movements you do not see but sense,
the drinking willows, the aimless dykes,
a dead-still town along the shore.

Give me the winter, the wasted landscape,
the field bereft of a sign of life,
the resilience of the crackling heather.

Give me the cat as he looks before
he leaps, leaps to fight, leaps to flee,
to mate or to hunt. As he looks.

Give me a horse in full gallop or
on his side in the grass. Give me

a question, no reply.

No More Suffering

There's no more suffering among mankind,
it's beer and skittles till deep into the night.
Grief is for tragic heroes, don't you know.

No, there's a great deal of happiness nowadays,
the sick old classics have had their day,
the secret idylls of Hermans, Lermontov, Céline.

'We had friends and they betrayed us,
we had lovers and they grew to hate us,
we have a cold fire burning in our breasts'.

It's as simple as that: out of the night
no man returns. Our dreams will all retreat
before the facts, never, never, the other way round.

An Empty Spot to Stay

Go now into the garden, dear, and lie
in an empty spot where the grass grows tall.
That's what I've always wanted to be,
an empty spot for someone, to stay.

Crow

Spring, now everything returns in me
I see that horse again too, that lies
with stretched-out legs, as though it were
dead with little wheels, see the grey
far too fat belly from which a crow
is picking fluff and hairs to build its nest.

She Waits

She waits with cooling tea and aging hands,
I love her, yes, but not with much

thirst or longing. Love is the end
of a quiet day, only the red in the sky

remains, the sun has set. She waits
and with the twilight comes the cat.

He thrusts his chilly back against her hands,
not for her sake, but for his fur's.

Slowly, in Drops

Over the roof the trees still bend
as bowed as grandmothers over a bed.

As we walk the rooms there's a muttering,
a sigh, a mumbling of prayers and stories.

Slowly, in drops, our names drip down
over the steamed-up window panes.

Here we have lived and here
we shall not come again.

Father, I See your Face

Father, I see your face again, years
after your death – almost a shadow
in this vastness, a shadow
white with heat – lonely
stone in the sky, the sea.

Head of a Roman general, nose
flattened, mouth torn open,
eye-sockets vacant, raised to
the sun, in a desert.

Almost a scream still at
this death.

Father, your face there, a sort of
island where no-one
has ever lived, where
no-one ever arrives.

Who Are You?

No face, no hands, no hair, and always someone
different. Again the odour of an unfamiliar coat,
as close as that odour, but as invisible too,
as much past and done. I look at the heath

at the misty, lonely birch-trees and ask myself
how must I say it, how must I say that?
I am happy again, just as alone again as before,
I longed, and did not know for whom. She

had no face yet, no hair, no hands, she was
always someone else, her odour was as close
but as strange as yours now. Who are you, I say,

we have a shared life behind us and still I have
to ask myself, dearest, who are you? She takes my head
in her hands and strokes the hair from my face.

He Knows Why

The back of a dog who already knows
as you stroke it that you're about to leave,
you stroke him, but he knows why.

I can see it – how slow you are becoming,
as though you have suddenly become very heavy,
that's how you slump away from my hand.

Later! Later? For you're already lying
as still as a dog can lie
in the sun.

You stroke, but
out of his back
comes no response.

Painting

1

Peaceful one, yet what sort of peace,
it is this stifling half-light, this room.
Beside the open window your silhouette and
myself here, who cannot see your face, I

who can only try to see what you
see: this grey sky, this empty square
among the crumbling houses, this small town
in which you lived, long before my time.

Your hand on the window-sill, your hand
in your lap, those hands that lie
as though they have received a letter,

but have not opened it
and will not either.

2

It is still this same sultry evening, and you,
I can't see your face, you are looking
away from me. I can see what
you see, I look through the open window

at the pale, hazy sky above the roofs,
the houses with their blank-eyed windows,
and down below the deserted square,
I look at your world, to see

your empty longing.

The way your head is turned, the way
your hands are laid there, the way
you sit, as though you had already
taken leave of your body.

3
You are looking out of the window at
the empty square below you, and I, I am
not there. I am here, behind you,
we never see each other, we keep looking

outside, as though at some moment, something
there might move, an inhabitant of this
blown flower of a town might come out
of some alleyway, like a cat, and he

does not come. We look, but never.

I can see your back. Because it is still
so young a back, I see how bent
it is, too still to say
a word to, too fragile
to do anything about.

4
Sick one, but what sort of sickness, look
at the grey sky, the shabby houses, the empty
square, there's nothing to be seen, behind secrets
there is no brain, no heart, there is no one.

Is this the moment after love departed
and left death behind with you, or is this
the moment before love was to arrive and
bring death with him, when is it?

Sick one, who am I who ask this, other
than the one who asks, this watcher?

It is nothing more than this painting, this
view of a view onto emptiness, this
repetition of questions, who
are you, who are you?

On a painting, *Teniers Square in Antwerp*, by Henry de Braekeleer (1840-1888)

Breughel's Winter

Winter by Breughel, the hill with hunters
and dogs, at their feet the valley with the village.
Almost home, but their dead-tired attitudes, their steps
in the snow – a return, but almost as

slow as arrest. At their feet the depths
grow and grow, become wider and further,
until the landscape vanishes into a landscape
that must be there, is there, but only

as a longing is there.

Ahead of them a jet-black bird dives down. Is it mockery
of this laboured attempt to return to the life
down there: the children skating on the pond,
the farms with women waiting and cattle?

An arrow underway, and it laughs at its target.

All Those Fine Promises

The green pastures, the still waters,
I have looked for them and indeed
have found them, they were even lovelier
than I had been promised,
magnificent.

And in this endearing landscape the son
of the maker, nailed to a tree,
but no trace of violence,
of resistance, just
peace, quiet.

His vacant eyes stare into the scene,
eternal questions play around his mouth,
why then, who are you,
where were you, and the like.

Without reproach, he must have known
what was about to happen.
I have no reply.

The Surveyor

It isn't mere indifference, in a certain sense
it is perhaps even love that drives him on,
there's no paradise without its steward.

He is happy with his landscape, but happy too
with searching, co-ordinates point him to his invisible
spot, the map, not the world, is his Utopia.

He wants to know where he is, but it's his consolation
to know that the spot where he is standing exists only
as his private formula, he is a hole in the shape of

a man in the landscape. With the boundaries that he draws,
sharper, more distinct, the grass and the trees grow
vaguer and everything that lives, declines and dies.

The world around him is perfectly clear, everything has been
    observed.

Conversation

1
The sound of goods trains, the old
stories of the night, that they're coming
to get you, that they'll take you with them,
but what remains is no more than
the rustling which is always there,

or the grey of a windstill sea in
the evening, perhaps beneath it there
is still a very slow breathing, yet
it is not to be seen, a sleep
so deep, so for ever, so long

as you live, something like that, she says, and I,
who have never wanted these talks, have never
had a reply, because I neither
can put a name to what I cannot hear
and do not see, but lie now

against her body, I think of her
as of a child that is a child no more,
of the old sounds of the night,
the colour of the old
summers by the sea.

2
Or that she says nothing, is simply dumb.
It is true, further and further away the gentle
goods trains vanish into the night,
they came to fetch me, I did not go, I stay
listening until I can hear no more.

That she is dead-still, it's as though she's asleep.
I see her lying, and indeed in her body lives
the secret of the swell
on a windstill sea, I stay
watching until I can see no more.

There is, I say, and think, there isn't.
The words with which I say: there was once
a time, and now it's past, there is a place
and this too has been deserted,
these are comfort, but why?

Not because of what has been, but because of
afterwards:
I hear, but the silence afterwards,
I see, but what is no more,
I think, but of what?

Onwards

1
From island to island, ever
smaller and sparser, across ever
vaster and wider waters, until
in the ultimate bay
the prospect completely
and finally opens out.

In this utterly indifferent world
strike sail.

2
Simply a landing-stage,
a few miserable houses,
a graveyard, a pub,
simply memories

of a gesture of faithfulness:
bed, glass and grave still
stand ready, against
all reason.

Go ashore here.

3
Night falls, but it is
as a bell of clouded glass,
already white from tomorrow's dawning.

They have gone before us
over this open, motionless sea.

Wait for the wind.

Suppose

1
Suppose that we could stay here –
but this prospect over the mountains
is too distant, too permanent
to be borne, although

if, in this attitude
we were to change into mountains,
we could stay lying here,

as accidental as all the rest.

2
So abandon people here,
the house, the table, the paper.

No return. This prospect.

3
In this attitude, as they lie
here, it seems perhaps
an attitude, it looks perhaps
like staying, but

whereas they rise up and
descend all around us, like
earthern bodies, asleep,

with the snow dripping off
their flanks and new falls
covering them again,

it is only as though we
could abandon ourselves,
invisible in this herd.

Further

1
Now we know we have lost our way
all we have left is this place.

Rain, to the horizon rain
and a sea of grey-green hills,
waves of wood after wood.

2
Our maps we have left behind,
somewhere, not angry, not wistful:

they told us what we already knew,
where we came from.
Not where we were.

3
Now on the point of going further
and not knowing how, not knowing

of the rustling, the fragrance, the darkness
under the trees, the screams
in the distance, the disappearing
tracks, not knowing what
anything means.

4
Our faces are taut and cold,
smoothed by the rain, as though we were weeping.

It is no weeping, it is
rain and skin.

5
Grey-green waves of wood after wood,
into those we shall disappear.

Out of those we shall return,
but it will no longer be us.

Who they are no-one knows.

In the Mountains

1
It exists, the almost being moved to tears,
for a moment as your eyes follow a track,
fall down and down
along a slope and arrive
in a hamlet,
deserted.

That stillness.

2
Already so far away that you no longer know
if the stones against the mountain are
still sheep, an avalanche
rolling slowly upwards
or already stones,

that you don't know what remains.

3
When you see what remains of it – you follow
a bird, the way he floats, strays
for a moment, falls, claps his wings,
catches the air again and
rises, rises –

not even the hole in the sky
through which he disappeared.

4
The idea of the perfectly open
ending, that something ceases even
before it ends,
disappears before it
has gone, is lying before
it lies down,

this exists.

A River

1
Mornings along the river, mornings when
it still seems to be considering
where it will go again
today,

whether it will make the same
violent motions it always has,
or now no more,

or are these endless vacillations
but the empty gestures of one
who no longer exists,

who has resigned himself

to being what he is, between his shores,
in the meaningless course
he has dug.

2
It's as though it wanted to begin again,
so restless seem its movements,
as though it could go back

to the country it came from,
back into its shadowy past

and then come here and lie down again,

but it is silent between
its shores, and its shores
are silent too.

3
As though it wanted to go further
than here, as though there's a destination,
a place somewhere
it has never yet been

and could get there,

but in the distance
it is already there – just as it
is here.

4
Morning along the river,
morning when at last
it will be no more than
a river.

Bay

It stays and it stays, it does not fade away:
a yellow beach with empty chairs,
a green and blue-green sea with little boats,
greyish mountains around it, and over all
a thin, lilac, coagulated light.

There was movement before, something was moving endlessly,
it was the breathing of the sea, the gentle rasp
of the little boats at anchor, the gradual
darkening and disappearance of the bay:
something was about to arrive and it came, it came,
this was happiness.

Something motionless remains, a moment in which
the beach has been deserted, the sea grows still,
the anchor chains fall silent, the light retains
that ancient lilac, and nothing disappears – moment
in which the bay lies as it is, forever,

and a longing for this moment to pass.

What I Said

1
What I said, let it become
natural, as natural
as leaves in the summer

   – then came the splendid misty
days when they began to fall,
or rather, they did not fall, they
loosened themselves, swayed in
not wind, yet something
that still endeavoured to bear their weight,
and lay down –

and as natural as their
dying, as the fragrance now
of winter, dead leaf, soil.

2
Let what I said lie
as snow lies, such as when
you get up and see it, ah,

   – it happened in the night,
while you lay here asleep,
there, outdoors, the world
was, flake by flake, transformed
into dead-silent snow –

and in the spring let it depart
as it came, as naturally,
let it, melting, murmuring, disappear.

The Valley

1
You see us again sitting in the grass;
those faces of ours, looking
as though they were seeing something
that makes them extraordinarily happy,

like the faces of the blind, unaware
of how they are seen, unsuspecting, looking
at their own secret.

In my notes you read very little
of this, I simply wrote:
been to the valley again, looked a long time,
it was still there.

2
And then you see again what
we were sitting looking at:
grey edge of the wood, the wickerwork
fencing drenched in twilight,
about us the very slightly undulating
soft-green meadows and in the hollow
the little row of spindly alders straying
along the invisible stream.

Then this is what must have made us
so extraordinarily happy.

3
You see how often these photographs have been
looked at, how often, too, the slip of paper
has been read, on which was written it was still there,
how spotted and thumb-marked they are.

That whole perfect world that must be
there – the wholly undiscoverable answer
to the question which world that is.

Natzweiler

1
And there, beyond the barbed wire, the view –
very charming landscape, as peaceful
as then.

They would need for nothing, they would
be laid down in those green pastures,
be led to those peaceful waters,

there in the distance. They would.

2
I trace the windows of the barrack huts,
watch-towers, gas-chamber.

Only the black reflection of distance
in the panes, of a peaceful landscape,

and beyond it, no one.

3
The dead are so violently absent, as though
not only I, but they too
were standing here,

and the landscape were folding their invisible
arms around my shoulders.

We need for nothing, they are saying,
we have forgotten this world,

But these are no arms,
it is landscape.

4
The yellowed photos in the display cases,
their faces ravaged by their skulls,
their black eyes,

what do they see, what do they see?
I look at them, but for what?

Their faces have come to belong
to the world, to the world
which remains silent.

5
So this is it, desertion, here is
the place where they took their leave,
far away in the mountains.

The camp has just been re-painted, in that gentle
grey-green, that gentle colour
of war,

it is as new, as though nothing
has happened, as though
it has yet to be.

Conversation with the Wanderer

What I want, he says, perhaps
I wanted to be a bird, a swallow
I saw, there, high in the mountains,
and wanted to stay there myself

in the shadow of the house by the river
where he nested, from where he flew up.

I remember the return,
the warm twilight on the terrace,
how I sat there, following the meanders
of the river into the fields, the hazy lines
of the mountains up into the distance,
the flight of a swallow –
until he disappeared.

I was tired and went up again in thought
into the mountains, higher and higher,
to that lonely, lucid world of rock,
sat there again in the wind and gazed
into the depths.

Perhaps, he says, I want something
I can look at for ever, that house
down there, the nest I have myself
deserted,

and the meanders of the river, the lines
of the mountains, laid still at last,

as it was there, the moment I
disappeared from view, something

that exists beyond myself.

I Cavalli di Leonardo

All those sketches he left behind –

endless series of repetitions: bunches of muscles, sinews,
knuckles, joints, the entire machinery
of driving-belts and levers with which
a horse moves,

and out of thousands of hair-thin little lines, the skin
almost invisibly gently disappearing into the paper
of ears and eyelids, nostrils,
skin of the soul –

he must have wanted to find out how a horse
is made and have realized
it can't be done,

how the secret of a horse grew and grew
beneath his pencil.

Made the most splendid designs, studied them,
discarded them.

Ghiberti's La Porta del Paradiso

Now, five centuries later, it is not old, it has
always been, will always be, what I suspected
that there was, a door to eternity.

The golden-yellow world I saw in the child's bible,
with Adam and Eve, Cain and Abel, Abraham and Isaac,
I see that it exists. This was the riddle,

that they loved and hated each other, that they were
able to; but it is true, it is a tale of old,
golden-yellow bronze, with no beginning, no end,

nothing is happening, only the shadows of the relief
move beneath the gradual shifting of the sun.

Michelangelo's David

Statues were not made, they had to be
'freed from the marble', as though they were
there already, always,

(somewhere, in a windless June, on a white
uninhabited island in a blue-green sea)

and he did indeed find a splendid stone,
under its skin a perfect machine
of brains, muscles and heart,

and no trace of effort, none of a movement
there had once been or still could be, simply
attitude, indifferent strength

of milliards of crystals, perfect
copy of a youth.

Michelangelo's Cristo Deposto di Croce

Old, 'so close to death, and so far from God',
he must have stood before this block of marble,

from which the splendid, youthful body of Christ
had already been released, though it hung limp

and dead in its mother's lap, and about
them an old man's arms, his face drained

of everything but grief, impotent ending,

his self-portrait. He had written: 'there is no
painting, no image now which sets the soul at rest,

the soul in search of divine love,
which opened its arms to us on the cross.'

He had wanted to be buried at the foot
of this statue, but smashed it and left

what remained of it ravaged, incomplete.

Rain and Wind

1
As though the house no longer exists

– when a child cried she took it
up and nestled it against her skin,
and hummed and crooned, her whole
body knew how it was done, how
it had to grow silent again. Then
the child was silent –

it surrounds us as naturally as that, we
have forgotten how it took us up
out of rain and wind.

2
As though the house no longer exists

– when he was dying he came and lay down
in this room, in this bed, here he
listened to the humming and crooning
of this house, the same sounds
we hear too now, still. Then
the house grew silent –

as naturally as that it finally lets us go,
it gives us back, we are forgotten
in rain and wind.

Afternoon in the Country

We looked him up – an afternoon like those that rise
time and again out of a well-thumbed page
of Chekhov, a languid country afternoon.

He led us through the ageing, patient house,
the garden with the ageing, patient apples, pears,
along the river and into the fields.

There we stood, he in that grey lounge suit,
that silk foulard, his cigar, man
of the world amid the buttercups.

Slowly, he said later in the shadow
of the trees on the terrace, I'm beginning to see
that this will be my home, my garden, forever.

Silence, warm and summery, scent of hay,
of ditches, sound of cattle tearing
at the grass, of passionately singing birds,

an afternoon as forever as a page.

Portrait

I
The longer it lasts, the longer
you love it, but what do you
love, it is changing
ever more into ever more
itself, so far into itself
it dies.

So alone will you become with love
as with a landscape
that is slowly changing into winter,
ever more into ever more
its one etching.

In your face still the face
that feels how warm breath is
before it cools into mist.

In your hand still the hand that tells
that you exist, until it
pulls back into your hand.

II
Now it is lying there, so withdrawn
into itself, so visible,
I know it's you no longer,
but what can I do?
It lies there and
I love it,

Lovable now, like a landscape in the winter
as it eventually reveals itself
in that last etching
of itself, what had to go
has gone.

In your face no longer a face, it is
white, like grass outside there, somewhere,
asleep and frosted with mist.

And the hand that told that you were there
has vanished into the hand that is lying
there, and is no more that hand.

Portrait with Bride and Bridegroom

They must have stood somewhere, naked
before the mirror, looked a last time at
their bodies, looked themselves in the eyes,
and taken their leave.

Now they are standing there, on the classical staircase,
between the classical pillars, everything in them is waiting,
waiting for what time is to do to them, a movement,
a tentative gesture, a glance.

There must be hands and eyes that know
how young and smooth her breasts are still, how touching
and flaccid his sex, how blind still their faces,
how it is still, like marble.

Portrait with Dog

That dog and I. He has withdrawn
into himself, and I

– I had laid my hand
on his back, his coat wrinkled,
I had looked into his eyes and he
stared up at my face as though
he was looking for something from my lips,
I had muttered something and
he laid himself down, sighed
and went to sleep –

I must have been something
in that hand, that face, those lips,

something I once knew, but that is now
hidden away in him, that dog.

Self-Portrait

As in the high windows of this house,
that's how it must be – as it is now.

It is evening, down there a few
ducks are floating on the pond, there
in the grass the path begins its long slow
upward arc through the wood, red
as stale blood, and above the hill
the heavens, dim with snow, mist
and smoke. There's a quacking, shrieking,
odour of wet leaves and wood fires,
it's cold to the cheek, that's

how it must be now, there. And no one
walking there, to hear all this,
to feel it, smell it. Shall we
draw the velvet curtains to
or leave them open?

Horses

Their nervous heads in the mist,
had I not known who they were,

I'd have thought it was no more
than the dream of being together

in a meadow in the winter,
but I knew, I recognized them.

They had come out of a past,
hesitated, and turned back into it.

Thanks to the Things

1
The morning when the things again come back
to life, when low light shines out of
the mahogany, table silver, porcelain,

the bread again begins to smell of bread,
the flowered teapot of tea,
the air of old people,

when, in the dead-still room, there comes
a muttering, Lord, bless this day too,
to all eternity, amen.

2
The afternoon when things again become
the afternoon, light flecks like butterflies
begin to dance in white and waving curtains,

the fruit bowl again begins to smell of fruit,
the chairs of cane, the bouquet in the vase
of lilacs, the flower-pot of earth,

when, in the dead-still verandah, knitting needles
begin to click, the newspaper to rustle again,
the gate squeaks, the gravel softly crunches.

3
The evening when the things again begin to long
to disappear, the red carpet, the brown
velvet curtains yearn for the darkness,

the pipe in the ash-tray smells again of smoke,
the banana of its fruity flesh, the milk
of the steaming milk of bedtime,

when, in the dead-still room, the Word
is heard again, the Book claps to,
silence falls again, the pendulum clock ticks.

4
The night when the things again begin to be
but shadows of themselves,

    the room again begins to smell of laundered sheets,
    old woodwork, lavender,

    when the dead-still window breathes again
    with sleeping treetops in the wind.

5
The moment when, call it
a morning, an afternoon,
an evening, a night,

    when the things begin again,
    call it a house where light,
    scents and sounds come
    and go,

    but it is death that is searching
    for words for the moment when
    I, and whatever he may say,
    I am that.